REAL PRAYERS FOR REAL PEOPLE

REAL PRAYERS FOR REAL PEOPLE

DAILY CONVERSATION STARTERS WITH GOD

Lucretia Mason-Underdue

Final Step Publishing, LLC
www.finalsteppublishing.com

Real Prayers for Real People – Daily Conversation Starters with God

Copyright© 2019 Lucretia Mason-Underdue

All rights reserved. This book is protected under the copyright laws of the United States of America. This book may not be copied or reprinted for commercial gain or profit. The use of short quotations or occasional page copying for personal or group study is permitted and encouraged. Permission will be granted upon request. All emphases within quotations are the author's addition.

Released – June 2019

Published by Final Step Publishing
P.O. Box 1447
Suffolk, VA 23439
www.finalsteppublishing.com

For Worldwide Distribution

Printed in USA.
ISBN: 978-1-7331469-9-9
Library of Congress Control Number: 2019911210

Praise for "Real Prayers for Real People"

Real Prayers for Real People is a "must read" for Christian believers seeking to strengthen their Christian prayer life. This powerful book is introspective and inspirational. Elder Mason-Underdue has provided meaningful and exemplary prayer models to use throughout your daily living. Read it for yourself, and as you are strengthened, "Let the redeemed of the Lord, Say So."

Bishop Curtis E. Edmonds, Sr.
Portsmouth, Virginia

Given the many challenges that we are prone to face in life, there is the constant need for renewal, reminders and revivals. That is precisely what Rev. Mason-Underdue, has done with this powerful prayer devotional. She writes out of her personal experience and allows the reader to peep into this tried and proven prayer time that is sure to energize, inspire and encourage. This is a must have for the seasoned believer, a newcomer to the faith, and the person who is seeking to have a deeper relationship with God. Get ready to be equipped to take on and tackle the daily demands of life with "Real Prayers for Real People."

Rev. Dr. Dwight Riddick, Sr.
Newport News, Virginia

I am very proud of you pursuing your dream. In a day wherein people are torn because of the unrest in our society, we need to know how they survive. It is through consistent prayer from real people. This is a must read for those who intend to survive spiritual warfare!

Rev. Dr. Lewis Watson
Salisbury, Maryland

The prayers are inspiring as well as encouraging. When I was reading each prayer, I could feel the passion that Elder Mason-Underdue felt as she talked to God. Without hesitation, I was encouraged to lean into the Lord closer. In "Real Prayers for Real People," there is certainly a powerful prayer that will renew and strengthen you morning, noon and night, from a heart bent towards God.

Elder Joyce Carcana
Portsmouth, Virginia

It is my prayer that "Real Prayers for Real People" will dethrone every false hope in your life and re-establish your understanding of sound, foundational, relevant prayers. I urge you to read it discerningly and allow Elder Underdue to help you restore the power and the practice of prayer as the focal point of your relationship with God. Do not let this book become just another resource manual but let it become a treasure chest, revealing in you the revelation of the Power of Prayer.

Bishop Landon B. Mason, Sr.
Hertford, North Carolina

Dedication

I dedicate this book to God, my Heavenly Father, who always assures me I can be an author of many books. To my dear husband, Clyde Underdue, I dedicate this book to you because of your unconditional love and support. I also dedicate this book to my late nephew, Alfred Davis, Jr. He would often say, "Aunt Cretia, I love to hear you preach because I can understand everything you say."

Acknowledgements

I am blessed beyond measure to have had a dedicated support team of individuals who have believed in me since the initial process of pursuing my first book. I would like to thank many people for their roles in bringing this book to fruition:

- My mother, Janice Butler, for raising me in a Christian environment and insisting that I and my siblings attend church on Sundays. For me, this is where it all started.
- All of my siblings: Lisa Brown, Lorraine Davis, Loren Mason, Landon Mason, Lynette Lyttle, and Lorita Peterson for the love and care extended to me while stepping out on faith.
- Thank you to my stepfather, Leroy Butler and my in-laws; Jeffrey Brown, Alfred Davis, Sr., Melvin Lyttle, Jr., Damon Peterson, and Maxine Mason for your ongoing support throughout my preaching ministry.

- To my Great-Grandmother, Celia Robertson, thank you who at ninety-three years old, continues to pray for me.
- My former pastor and First Lady whom I affectionately call, "Da" and "Ma," Bishop Curtis Edmonds, Sr. and Lady Evelyn Edmonds, for your spiritual guidance and for giving me the opportunity to exercise my gifts and talents in the church. Thanks for also taking me under your wings as a daughter to whom you continually show love.
- My loving nieces and nephews who always have words of encouragement for me and remind me that I can do anything I set my mind to do.
- My Pastor and First Lady, Rev. Dr. Dwight Riddick, II and Rev. Dr. Jennell Riddick for motivating me when I first mentioned I wanted to write a book.
- Andrea, Aaron, and Alexia Burford for supporting me in all I do and encouraging me to finish this book.
- Elder Joyce Carcana for embracing my ideas and then asking, "What are you waiting for?" after having a conversation about writing a book. You also took me in as a niece, friend, and dear sister in the ministry.
- My mentor, Sheila Hunt, for opening many doors in my life and reinvigorating me to pursue this book.
- Rev. Dr. Dwight Riddick, Sr. and Rev. Dr. Lewis Watson for also being spiritual fathers and believing in me.
- Dr. John Kinney, for allowing me to begin this book in an independent course when enrolled at Samuel Dewitt Proctor School of Theology at Virginia Union University. Now, Dr. Kinney, it has come to fruition!

Table of Contents

PRAISE FOR "REAL PRAYERS FOR REAL PEOPLE"

DEDICATION

ACKNOWLEDGMENTS

TABLE OF CONTENTS

PREFACE I

MORNING PRAYERS 3

AFTERNOON PRAYERS 25

NIGHT PRAYERS 49

EIGHT PRAYER STARTERS 73

HELP ME MAKE IT THROUGH SCRIPTURES 79

Preface

Pray! Why pray? Prayer is our way as Christians to communicate with God, our Heavenly Father. When we pray, God appreciates it, and He loves it when we are real while talking to and with Him. As we converse with God, let us not forget that God wants to communicate back to us. When this takes place, prayer is no longer a monologue, but it becomes a dialogue; you talk to God and God talks to you.

Growing up in a Christian environment introduced me to my prayer life. Before leaving home to go to school, my mother required family prayer. Also, before going to church, once again, my mother required us to pray. When I was growing up, prayer was essential in our home, and now that I am an adult, prayer continues to be just as important.

God wants us to communicate with Him because prayer is the connection that brings the relationship between man and God together. Communication is the key to any relationship; husband and wife, parent and child, aunt and uncle, family and friend, supervisor and employee, professor and student, store clerk and customer, teacher and parent, doctor and patient, and the list goes on. If communication does not take place in the above-mentioned relationships, there will not be a connection between the two individual, and the relationship will remain undeveloped. However, when communication takes place, things begin to change, and the relationship has not been neglected or ignored. It would benefit us if we were to think on that same level when identifying our relationship with God. It takes communicating with him through prayer in order for our relationship to move forward in a progressive manner.

If you will allow yourself to think about past relationships and the lack of communication that took place, what were the results? Now think about past relationships where communication was key, and it took place on a daily basis. What were the results? The relationship when communicating regularly may not have always resulted in your favor, but the outcomes took place because of effective communication. As Christians, we should not treat God any less than our earthly companions. If we want to maintain a close relationship with God, we should make daily communication with Him a mandate. We are required to read our Bibles, to have faith, and yes, to pray to an Almighty God who is willing, able, and ready to answer our prayers.

If we were to be completely honest with ourselves, we all have fallen short when it comes to communicating with God. The question is, "How do you think we made Him feel?" How did we feel when our love ones did not communicate to us? We probably did not like it. Some of us became angry or upset and some of us held a grudge that we refuse to let go until this day. Let us be reminded that God is our loved one also, and he loves us so much that he allowed his only begotten son, Jesus Christ, to die for us all.

LUCRETIA MASON-UNDERDUE

The least we can do is to put forth an effort to pray more, communicate with him, and allow him to communicate with us. This book can help in many ways to strengthen your prayer life. It consists of sixty prayers from the heart, and they are categorized in three different ways: morning, afternoon, and night prayers. You do not have to read a morning prayer in the morning because you may be led to read a morning prayer at night. Guess what? It is fine to read any prayer at any time because you may be experiencing morning at night. Regardless of when you pray each prayer, know that God is listening intently and cherishes your time together. And most of all, may you be blessed.

Morning Prayers

Prayer for the Day

Dear Lord, as I begin my day I have no idea what will take place. My greatest blessing is knowing who holds this day. It's you, dear God, and therefore I have no reason to fear because you will be with me just like you were with me last night as I slept. As I begin to give it deeper thought, you have never failed me, and your track record proves you will never leave me. I am beginning to rejoice after reminding myself that you've got the whole world in your hands. No matter what comes and no matter what goes, I am believing that nothing will take place today without you having known about it. It's going to be a great day because I have spoken it into existence. In Jesus' name I pray, Amen.

Prayer to Say Thank You Lord

As I meditate on your goodness, I cannot contain myself. You are so good to me, and I do not deserve your blessings. All I can say this morning is thank you, Lord! I have asked for many things from you, but today I just want to say thank you! I need to worship, thank, and praise you more because I do not do it as often as I should. You have never failed me. When I thanked others and put others before you, for some reason you still blessed me. Please forgive me, Lord God, I will do better because you deserve better. In Jesus' name I pray, Amen.

A Closer Connection

It is me again, God. Another morning, another reason to praise you, and another reason to call upon your holy and righteous name. I pray for a closer walk with you in every decision that will be made today. Yes, I know if I can stay connected with you throughout this day, it will be fruitful and prosperous. You have carried me through my roughest days, and you have stood with me through my joyous moments. It is because of the many days I have already trusted and encountered you, today will be no different. I am trusting our connection will get closer and closer as I keep my mind focused on you. In Jesus' name I pray, Amen.

A Closer Connection

Oh God, I am grateful for the moon, stars, and the sky. You created it all. The clouds, grass, and trees were also part of your creation. You, Father God, are the creator of the universe, and your creation is so amazing. No man can claim the creation of this world because your plans have always been beyond what man could ever think or imagine. I had absolutely nothing to do with this marvelous creation of a world, and yet, you did not forget to create me in your own image. I am blessed to be a part of your creation because when you created me, you stated it was very good! I know that I am only a resident with a temporary lease here on this earth, so I will not ever think to make it my permanent home. Thank you, Lord, for including me and not excluding me. Thank you for handcrafting me, for I am wonderfully made. Hallelujah! In Jesus' name I pray, Amen.

God's Goodness

Dear God, thank you for always being there for me. You are my everlasting joy. There are no words adequate to describe your goodness toward me. Your works are indescribable. Again, I say thank you, Lord. Every now and then, my heart begins to flood with tears because you are so good to me and my family. Please help me to stay the course as I follow your directions. Also help me to be humble. I want so much to be more like you as I think about the many examples that you have provided for me. You are so great and powerful. I love you, God. This is my prayer in Jesus' name, Amen.

Bless Someone Today

Dear God, I want to live today in a way that I will be a blessing to someone else. I want to bless someone with a smile, an encouraging word, or even a monetary donation if it be your will. You have blessed me in various ways, and you have created me to also be a blessing to others. Help me to reach the unreachable and bless that person who stands in the need of a blessing. Whether it be big or small, lead me to draw someone closer to you because of the way they will be blessed. By the way, God, thank you for pouring out blessing after blessing in my life. In Jesus' name I pray, Amen.

Moving Forward

Good morning, God, I know that I have been holding back from moving forward in life. Please forgive me. At this point I am asking you to send me and I will go! I have been slipping lately, and now it is time for me to move forward. I refuse to remain stagnant when you have positioned me to "GO!" I became complacent and comfortable, which caused me to sit when you commanded me to move. Now I realize, God, that there is more in store for me, if I would just move when you give me the green light. I have been sitting at this red light for quite some time. Thank you for setting me up to stand and not fall. It has never been because of you that I am not where I should be right now. It is indeed me. I have to also thank you for being patient with me, God, and for never giving up on me like I have given up on myself in the past. I am moving now, Lord, thanks to you. In Jesus' name I pray, Amen.

Peace

Dear God, as I prepare myself for today I ask for peace in every situation. Please help me to shift my thinking, slow down, and completely give this day to you. Help me to only take a glimpse of yesterday so I will be empowered to follow your leadership even more today. I need that peace that will surpass all understanding, God, because that is the type of peace that will calm every storm. It will help me cross every valley and to understand that which others cannot comprehend. For that is the kind of peace that will only come from you. I claim peace now, Lord, in Jesus' name I pray, Amen.

Thank You, Lord

Dear God, when I think of you, I have to thank you. How often have I forgotten to tell you thanks? If I were to count my blessings, I would run out of numbers, because that is just how great you have been to me. When I did not know which way to go, you always took the wheel. How much does it cost just to say thank you? How much does it cost just to call on your name? If there was a price to pay, would I be rich, or would I be in debt? I am increasing my prayer life as of today, God, not only asking for something, but to also say thank you! In Jesus' name I pray, Amen.

A Great Day

My God, it is going to be a great day! I feel it! This is a day that absolutely nothing or no one will be able to take from me. I wish I had this mindset every morning because this is what is needed for spiritual warfare. I am girded this morning with the full armor of God, ready for battle, and filled with his spirit from above. For this is the day that you have made, God, and I will rejoice and be glad in it! Thank you for showing me that weapons will form today but by no means will they prosper. This is your word, God, and I am walking in it today and the days to come. In Jesus' name I pray, Amen.

From a Good to Greater Day

Dear God, I am waking up with you on my mind. Yesterday was beyond good, and today will be even better. I am prepared for the best to come because I know that I can count on you. I am praying for every person that I will come into contact with today because they need you like I need you, whether they realize it or not. It is because of you that we all have made it this far in our lives. You are great and greatly to be praised! Please allow my spirit to be in an attitude of prayer throughout this day because I just cannot make it without you, God. Therefore, my hope is in you and my praises will go to you. It is you who is truly worthy to be praised. In Jesus' name I pray, Amen.

The Next Chapter in Life

Dear God, the more I think about what my future holds, the more I have to cling to you, Lord, for what lies ahead. I am trusting you to open the next door and carry me to the next chapter of my life's story. God, you are my publishing company, and I will not be able to complete another chapter without your approval. I need you to show me, God, and confirm in me what you would have me to do and which way you want me to go. I live for you. In Jesus' name I pray, Amen.

Still Standing

Dear God, I rose this morning because I continue to exist, and it is all because of my source, which is you. Oh God, you are my source and my strength. It is because of you that battles are won in my life. Forever I will be a soldier in your army. I got through boot camp because I was able to persevere with power from you. I was able to stand after being on the front line of life, and you captured my enemies when they tried to take me down. Thank you, God, for shielding me. You are my all and all. Thank you for being my all and all. In you I put my trust and gain strength. I realize now as I did then that I still cannot make it on my own. Please, God, keep me in your care because your care is like no other. In Jesus' name I pray, Amen.

Purpose

Oh God, I know you are alive. I am not fully awake, but I am getting there because you are alive in me. If you did not live in me, I would not be here today. I would not be afforded this thing we call life, health, or well-being. I really need to be singing and rejoicing even now because of LIFE! God, you sent Jesus so we may have life and have it more abundantly. That is awesome news to me. I am so glad you know what to do and I am at an advantage because you do all things well. With that being said, I ask that you show me my purpose in life and help me to live in a God-fearing manner, so others may look at me and see you. I declare and decree that my life is completely in your hands. This is my prayer in Jesus' name I pray, Amen.

Lifting Up God's Name

Dear God, I am awake, and that is a good reason to lift my hands and praise you. It is early and my day is already complete in you. I have to be truthful, God. I do not feel this good every day, but it is engraved in my mind who woke me up this morning. When I arose, I did not have any doubt that you would be God and that you would continue to claim me as one of your own. This makes it an outstanding morning, knowing I have Your DNA. Thank you, God, for showing me that I am unstoppable, and I can do all things through you who will give me the strength I need to complete any task that comes before me this day. Alright, God, walk with me as I take each step in a day that belongs to you. This is my prayer in Jesus' name, Amen.

Healing for My Body

Dear God, I am not feeling well this morning because my body is weak. Please touch me, God, and bring healing into this body you created. I need your healing power to take complete control because I believe in you and your mighty power. I have known you to be a healer and I know you can do just that, if it is your will. A touch from you makes all the difference in the world. I am not complaining; I am just making a request known unto you. In Jesus' name I pray, Amen.

Moody Morning

Dear God, thank you for allowing your son to shine on me this morning. Since I am not in the best mood, I give myself to you so my morning will go in another direction. I know when I am more attentive to you, my days are lighter, and my direction is much clearer. Help me, God, to press on in spite of my mood and to praise you for another day that was gifted to me. All of my mornings are not like this one, and through you I will still prosper. In Jesus' name I pray, Amen.

No Complaining

Good morning, God. Today is not a day that I will resort to complaining about anything. I just want this day to be filled with distributing love from me to others because you are love. I want this day to go as planned by you, Heavenly Father, because you have the master plan unlike any other blueprint. For this reason, I say that I am yours, Lord. Use me for your glory and keep me from complaining on this Christian journey. Better yet, increase my praise unto you. In Jesus' name I pray, Amen.

Relationship

Dear God, because you know me, you already know my thoughts this morning. I need help with this relationship that is burning me out. I seek your help because there is no one else to rely on like you. I do not want to begin my day worrying about something that I need to give completely to you. Please, God, take what may hinder me from having a productive and blessed day. I take my hands off and ask that you wrap me in your arms and tell me what I need to do. Show me what decisions you want me to make according to your will. In Jesus' name I pray, Amen.

Afternoon Prayers

Communicating with God

Dear God, it feels good to communicate with you midday. It was you who carried me through my morning, and now you are making for certain that I am covered this afternoon. I would not trade you for anything in this world because of who you are to me. Now continue what you have started in me, so I may enter my night with joy in my heart. In Jesus' name I pray, Amen.

It's Rough Lord

Right now, Lord, this mountain in my life looks as though it's just too high to climb, and the waters I am swimming in are extremely deep. Whatever the case may be, Lord, I can rest assured that you will not allow me to be destroyed. However, you will set me in a position to be restored while climbing this mountain. Even when I am in the deep waters, you are my lifeguard who will not allow me to drown. You constantly remind me that the deep waters are there only to cleanse me. Thank you, Lord, for allowing my life to rest in the bosom of your arms where I am safe. You are such an awesome God! You watch over me like a good shepherd who watches over his sheep and causes them to lie down safely in green pastures. In Jesus' name I pray, Amen.

Trusting God

An inward change is what it took for me to move forward according to your plan. I am willing to continue to move because I trust that you will continue to order my steps, Lord. For I have learned that when I order my steps, I always fail miserably! When I march to the beat of your drum, every move is sharp and in tune. You are truly my song, Lord. You are forever whispering melodies of promises in my ear as I continue to march to the beat of your drum. Yes, Lord, I will forever trust you. Your song will always be music to my ears. In Jesus' name I pray, Amen.

Tested and Tried

Dear God, even now please teach me how to believe you have a perfect plan for me when I cannot see it. This afternoon I have been tested and tried. Things do not appear to be working in my favor, but I serve you, God, and that makes all of the difference in the world. I am stepping out and still believing in you and your word, knowing that this, too shall pass. In Jesus' name I pray, Amen.

Think Positive

Dear God, please allow me to think on those things that are pure, righteous, and holy. I do not want to cause anyone to stumble. Put a bridle on my tongue, God, and allow me to only speak when you see fit. I want to represent you well by showing godliness toward others even when it's not shown to me. In Jesus' name I pray, Amen.

Faith

Faith is what's needed to please God. This Christian journey is a faith walk. I was not here when Jesus died, but I believe it by faith. This same faith is used to increase my daily walk in you, Lord. Today, I feel as though my faith is much larger than the grain of a mustard seed. Whatever problems arise, by faith I've already received the victory. I walk by faith and not by sight. My life is seen through the lens of faith, and for this reason, I will continue to be a faith walker. In Jesus' name I pray, Amen.

Blessings

Dear God, I come to you this afternoon with a glad heart. You continue to bless me in ways I will never understand. You continue to look beyond my faults and recognize my every need. You are a God that has never and will never fail me. Since the day that I made Jesus my choice, you have made me your choice. Your blessings are unforgettable and unending. Thank you, God! I will forever keep my trust in you. In Jesus' name I pray, Amen.

Rejoicing

Dear God, I am rejoicing because I can now see the light at the end of the tunnel. I knew this day would come and it did not take long. My weeping endured for a night, but now here it is noon, and I have joy as though it is morning. Everything is happening in your timing, which is far better than mine. You are so amazing, God. Just amazing! Please do not ever take your hands off of me. In Jesus' name I pray, Amen.

Growing Pains

Dear God, you are growing me. It does not always feel good, but I know it will work out for my good. I always feel as though you know what is best for me, and my inner self wants what is best because my life lies in your hands. Oh, how blessed I am because the one who knows me best has my interest at heart. While experiencing these growing pains, I am holding on to your promises. I am also a firm believer that there is a promise for every pain and a solution for every struggle. I am leaning on you for this one, too. In Jesus' name I pray, Amen.

Go to the Rock

Dear God, if it had not been for you on my side this afternoon, I do not know where I would be. God, you fill the shoes that no one else can walk in. You remind me often that I am your child, and that I am a conqueror regardless of my circumstance or situation. Please keep doing what no person can do in my life but you. Your kindness and genuine heart surpasses all. I am led to the rock on a day like today, one that is higher than I. I will keep coming to the rock, and that rock is you, dear God. In Jesus' name I pray, Amen.

Great God

My afternoon is going so well, dear God, and I am basking in your goodness for all you have done. You have held true to your promises. Oh, how great you are! When I feel myself falling, you pick me up. When I feel myself drowning, you become my lifeguard. When I feel myself not knowing which way to turn, you become my Map Quest. What more can I ask? Nothing. Thank you, God, for being in my life. In Jesus' name I pray, Amen.

Feeling Good

Oh God, what a breathtaking afternoon! I feel good because my mind is focused on you! Absolutely no one makes me feel the way that you make me feel. When I am lonely, you comfort me, and when I am hurt you heal me. I have become speechless at this point because my focus continues to remain on how good you really are to me. I thank you, God! In Jesus' name I pray, Amen.

Thank You

In the middle of the day I wanted to pause and say, "Thank you, Lord." I did not pay for my health, and I did not have to pay for my strength. It was all free from you to me. I did not have to pay for my life because Jesus Christ took on that expense. In you, my debt has been paid and the least I can do now is tell you again, "Thank you, Lord." It's all paid, and I owe my life to you. In Jesus' name I pray, Amen.

God, You are Worthy

Dear God, how can I repay you for your mighty acts? When I look at my surroundings, I see your mighty hand. When I look in the mirror, I see your mighty works. I am so unworthy of your acts of love. If I have not always appreciated you like I was supposed to, please forgive me. You are beyond worthy of all the glory and all of the honor. In the noonday, I can still lift my hands and give you the praise you deserve and then some. Thank you, God, for allowing me those few moments to look back, in order to bring me forward. In Jesus, name I pray, Amen.

Low on Finances

Dear God, for some reason I am thinking about my unpaid bills. Help me to worry less and pray more. Please touch my bank account and multiply it in some way. I need to hear from you now, God, because I honestly do not have the money, but I can still rejoice in knowing my account is in your hands. Give me what I need to continue my day as if my bills have already been paid. I am trusting in you to turn things around. You have done it for others, and I am believing you can do it for me. In Jesus' name I pray, Amen.

Feed Me, God

Dear God, I was waiting for this lunch break because I need to be fed, refreshed, and restored by you. Your promises are true, and I know that the blood will never lose its power. At this time, I pray that you will allow your Holy Spirit to increase and allow me to decrease. You are my real lunch break, God, and I can count on you to feed me the right food, so I may remain healthy in you. Take away my appetite for the junk food that destroys my connection with you. I am counting on you to feed me the fruit of the spirit that will help me to live more for you. This is my prayer in Jesus' name, Amen.

Prayer for a Friend

Dear God, I am calling on you because I know you can help my friend who is in distress. My friend is facing hardships and battling depression. My friend is very private and does not like to discuss personal business with others. Only you can help my friend, God, to overcome these obstacles. I am asking and pleading with you to take control and show my friend there is a better way found in you. In Jesus' name I pray, Amen.

God's Benefits

Oh God, here I am expressing how appreciative I am for another afternoon that you have blessed me to see. I have been very busy, God, as you already know, but I have not forgotten to pray. Your handprint surrounds me and serves as a reminder that I need to pray and remember all of your benefits. Your benefits package is second to none, and your childcare does not compare to any other. Thank you, God, for your continued benefits that I did not earn, and yet you freely give. In Jesus' name I pray, Amen.

LUCRETIA MASON-UNDERDUE

Prayer for the Country

Dear God, I pray for the United States of America. I lift up our president, who needs you, your wisdom, and guidance. Please God help the president to lead your country in a better way for your people. We belong to you. Besides you, there is no other that can make things better for a country that states, "In God we trust." I am trusting you, God, and believing that you will make things alright. We say that we are the United States, God. Please help us all to embrace unity and put a special touch on our president. In Jesus' name we pray, Amen.

Patience

Oh God, my God, I am blessed to know I can call on you midday. You have proven time and time again that you are a twenty-four-hour God who never sleeps or slumbers. I know you are listening to me even now. Help me to have more patience with others, especially those in whom I come in contact with on a daily basis, including my family members. I am weak in this area of my life and will lean on you to help me make it through. I need to do better in that department of my life. Help me, Lord God. In Jesus' name I pray, Amen.

Treat Others God's Way

Dear God, please help me on my job this afternoon. I want to do good, but evil truly besets me on every hand. I am not treating others right, although they are not treating me right either. I cannot fall into that trap of repaying evil for evil. Help me to treat others the way you have it outlined in your word, which includes treating them with love even when I am persecuted. God, you know it is not easy for me to do that, but I am willing to keep trying until I get it right. Please work with me God, so you can get the glory from this, too. In Jesus' name I pray, Amen.

Night Prayers

Healing and Strength

Strength is what I need, oh Lord, for I am weak. It is only through you that I shall gain strength. Your help is what I desire, and your help is what I seek. As I am being tried at this point in my life with challenge after challenge, I need you to uphold me with your righteous right hand. I know you are able to guide me through this, for you are my biblical navigational device. I am trying so hard to follow your directions so I won't get lost in the pain but find peace while resting in your presence. Heal and strengthen me, God, like only you can. In Jesus' name I pray, Amen.

God is Closer than a Friend

Dear God, the closer I get to you, the more I realize no friend compares to you. It is you, God, who is the true meaning of a friend.

A friend in you is what I've found,
When everyone else that was around,
Left me without notice and without a plan,
This is when I decided to put my trust in no man.
I am convinced as of today,
After all I've been through, I'd rather do it your way.
For so long I was wrong, it's not about them and it's not about me.
It's really all about you and glorifying your name,
Doing it this way, my life will never be the same.
So it's you I lift up, my Lord, my friend,
You've proven to stick closer than a brother, and you'll go with me till the end.

LUCRETIA MASON-UNDERDUE

You are my definition of a friend. Lord, you are the only one who thought so much of me that you laid down your life. There is no greater friend, and there is no greater love than your love for me.

Resting in God

Dear God, it is going to be a good night because I realize you are my creator and you will always keep me safe. Resting in your arms is what I need at the end of the day to get me through the night. Oh, what peace surrounds me as I rest in your arms. Resting in you brings, not only peace, but comfort, and now I feel like going on. My night is complete as I swim through the night because you are my Life-Savior! In Jesus' name I pray, Amen.

Trust the Process

Dear God, although it is my bedtime, I am in need of your help. I know you would tell me to trust the process because you are in it. Then you would continue to let me know that, regardless where you lead me, I need to just trust the process. I know you can be trusted, but I have this doubt sometimes that wants me to believe nothing good will come out of this process. So, help me, God, because all of my help comes from you. When I want to turn left and you want me to go right, please help me, God. When I get weary in well doing, please prop me up so I can remain in the race. In Jesus' name I pray, Amen.

Moving Forward

Dear God, I am pondering over my day and all I can say is that, "I am doing the best I can. I've moved five feet forward and ten feet backwards." Is this really a setback? Or is this a setup for a combat designed by you, God? Shall I keep on moving and realize the setback is going to work out for my good? What should I do, Lord? I cannot stay in this place forever because I cannot allow this one thing to hold me back. Help me, God, to move forward in Jesus name. I need your help and I cannot take one more step without you. I am on the verge of turning backwards because it feels like a much safer place. Push me, Lord. Take charge because your plan is a lot better than mine. In Jesus' name, Amen.

Rejoicing in the Rain

Dear God, even at night, the rain is continuing to fall into my life; drip drop, drip drop. What must I do when it is bedtime and I cannot sleep? I know, God, I can continue to pray because the rain helps me to make it to my next level in life. If I did not have any rain, God, I would not be able to grow in you. Thank you, God, for helping me to see that I will not reach my full potential without the rain and the sun. I ask that you take me by my hand and help me to allow the rain to fall as you continue to be the umbrella in my life. Please ease my mind, God, because you are the real weatherman who knows when it will rain and when the sun will shine. You never get the forecast wrong, God. For this I am ecstatic. This is my prayer in Jesus' name I pray, Amen.

Family

Dear God, I come to you tonight, thanking you for my family that you have blessed me with in this lifetime. You have supplied our needs and you have also given us the desires of our heart. Help us to remain unified and to connect with you daily. When we are not near each other, please help us to do the right thing around other people so you will be praised. I know family is important in the body of Christ, so I ask for more of you in our lives. We are not the perfect family, but we are a godly family because of your saving grace. Thank you, God, and please hear this prayer in Jesus' name. Amen.

Fallen Short

Dear God, as I prepare for bed, I am thinking about the fact that I am your child after your very own heart, but like David I fall short, too. I ask that you forgive me for my sins that have caused me to stumble today. I pray that tomorrow will show more of your character in me. If you were not a forgiving God, my life would not be worth living. I could not have gone to bed with things such as that on my heart because you have been exceptional in my life and deserve better from me. Now I can close my eyes tonight with a smile on my heart because you forgave me. Oh what a peaceful night God has planned for me. Thank you, God. In Jesus' name I pray, Amen.

Rest

Dear God, I am about to roll over in this bed you have blessed me with for comfort and rest. Today was a good day, and tonight will be better because I stand in the need of rest. So often I find myself not getting adequate sleep, but tonight, God, I thank you for allowing me to get more rest than I would have normally gotten. It feels really good to have had a productive day and to know a more restful night is ahead. Even you rested on the seventh day, God. Also help me to be more obedient to you, so I may rest more like this in the future. Then I will have more energy to give you the praise. In Jesus' name I pray, Amen.

Fully Covered

Dear God, I am having some good thoughts as I lay here in this bed. I can relax in knowing that everything is going good, God, because you are my assurance and my insurance. I stand as one who can rest knowing that you are my source and key to life. What a wonderful feeling! The insurance policy the world offers can't compare to your 100% coverage. Your plan is better because I am fully covered with benefits literally out of this world! Thank you, Jesus, for paying my deductible and for overriding my premium! This is my prayer in Jesus' name I pray, Amen.

God Gets the Credit

Another day complete and I made it through because of you! I am confident in knowing that by faith, mountains can move, and if the mountain refuses to move, you will give me strength to climb like you did today. My days of completion are because of you, and you do all things well. The more mature I become in you, God, the more I count my blessings. When I begin to think, I begin to thank. I thank you for all you have done for me this day and every day. The credit belongs to you, and all to you I owe. In Jesus' name I pray, Amen.

God's Goodness

Dear God, as I conclude another day, I meditate on how good you were to me. Every question was answered, and every move was positive. I have you to thank for that because you led me, and I followed. You are my everlasting joy, peace, and love. I pray for more days like this one because my load was lighter, and my day was brighter. I will continue to follow as you lead. I will continue to go and grow in you. I have learned to meditate on more of your goodness because the good has outweighed the bad. As I continue to prepare for a good night's rest, may you lay beside me and catch me when I roll over so I will not fall. In Jesus' name I pray, Amen.

Help Me and My Tongue, Oh God!

Dear God, I know I can be myself and admit my faults to you. Well, I have to admit my tongue caused damage today, although I tried very hard to manage it in a good way. My words were said in such a distasteful manner, and I ask for forgiveness. I realize the tongue is small but powerful. I try fixing the words I say, but my way has yet to work. I now give my thoughts, mind, and words to you God, because I know you will do a much better job than I will. Help me to use my tongue to bless and not to curse, to speak life and not death, to encourage and not to harm. Help me, Lord, to embrace a new beginning tomorrow morning when you allow me to awaken. Please take control of my tongue, my night, and the rising of my incoming day. In Jesus name I pray, Amen.

Availability to God

I am available to you,

I am willing to do what you would have me to do.

Use me as you see fit,

I am only straps without you, and I need you to knit,

Knit me together and mold me for your good,

I want to live my life for you just like I know I should.

I am available to you,

I am surely your child,

With you as my guide, I can go that extra mile.

No Complaining

Oh God, life is so good as I concentrate on keeping you in the forefront of my journey. I do not have a reason or a right to complain because you sent us your only son. You did not complain, but you freely gave. Who am I to even think about complaining when you have allowed my heart to beat all day long and my mind to think all day long? Every thought was not right, but you continued to spare my life. You have proven your love for me over and over again. As I lay my head down to sleep, I smile before I close my eyes. I am smiling because of your love that cannot compare to any other love. It's unconditional. Just when I think I am at my worst; you love me regardless. Is there anyone else who can love me like you can? No, because your love will never stop, and for this reason alone, I will not complain. In Jesus' name, good night and Amen.

Feeling Your Presence, Lord, In the Struggle

Dear God, somewhere in the world today, you allowed the birds to chirp and the winds to blow. This, God, is proof of your presence. I must admit that it is good to feel the wind, but it is better to feel your presence. Holy Spirit reign down on me because now is the time that I need to feel you the most. Life today was something else. It was a struggle, but you got me through it. I'm depleted, Lord, but I have enough strength to call upon your name. Oh, how sweet your name is as I whisper it now. Wrap my mind around nothing but you and cover me like I know you will. Oh, thank you, Lord God. Your presence is all around. My focus is you. I know, Lord, that the wind would not blow, and the birds would not chirp without you. I also know that I could not feel your presence without you in my life. Without your presence I am like a ship without a sail. Thank you, Lord, for the birds, the wind, but most importantly for your presence. My focus is still you, and it has made my struggle less stressful. In Jesus' name I pray, Amen!

My Home

Dear God, it's another night, and for some reason I am still here. My heart has become joyful as I get in bed and think about my next home. I know that heaven will be my eternal home, and hell has no place in my heart. I have been promised a mansion, and a mansion I shall receive. As you prepare my heavenly home, give me strength to help me keep my earthly home intact. Every now and then my home gets dirty, but you are my spiritual cleaner. You do not leave trails of dust or dirt behind. You never cease to amaze me, God, you are just that good! Good night. We will talk in the morning. This is my prayer, in Jesus' name, Amen.

Ticket to Heaven

Tonight, God, and for the rest of my life, I will proclaim this faith journey as my ticket into heaven flying first class. No one else can convince me otherwise. I'll awake in the morning seeing with 20/20 spiritual vision, and I'll retire for the night knowing I have a great optometrist who declares I don't have to wear bifocals on this Christian journey. I have perfect vision seeing how you'll master every detail of my life because I belong to You, Lord. Thanks for the reminder that I have been exempt from future eye exams and for this reason, I am grateful. I see with advanced vision that you'll never leave me nor forsake me. When I rise through the storms of life, I can tell myself, "God's got me." How do I know? I see it, before I see it! Thank you, God. This is my prayer in Jesus' name I pray, Amen.

Leaning on God

Dear God, learning to lean on you has not always been completely easy but it has been totally worth it. I am trusting you again tonight to turn things around because you are the captain of my soul. With you there is no sinking, drowning, or jumping overboard. With you onboard the ship, I can be certain that it may endure some rough waves, but at some point, it will be steady. Thank you for taking this day and ensuring within my heart that whatever came toward me, did not catch you by surprise. Truthfully speaking, you had already taken care of it, so I thank you for handling this day, too. In Jesus' name I pray, Amen.

When Your Plans for the Day Fail

Dear God, absolutely nothing went as I planned today. If I had to do it all over again, I would have prayed to you earlier and asked for your help. Now I know, God, that I should seek you in the morning and throughout my day. For some reason, God, I am still believing there was purpose in today not going according to plan. I can rejoice in knowing that at the end of the day, you are still God. After all, it was you who gave me strength to breathe fresh air, a voice to talk, and to also say that I am alive because of you. Before I close my eyes, I make this promise to you, dear God. I will begin and end my day with you because you indeed are my life-support. This is my prayer in Jesus' name I pray, Amen.

LUCRETIA MASON-UNDERDUE

Eight Prayer Starters

LUCRETIA MASON-UNDERDUE

The number eight denotes a new beginning. Here are eight prayer starters to begin your new and/or improved prayer life. Below are meditative thoughts that will result in prayer.

I. "Why wouldn't you put all of your trust in me after all I've done for you?"

Take time to meditate on how you need to trust God in all circumstances. Pray and ask him to help you trust him more.

Prayer Results:

_____

_____

_____

II. "Why not you?"

Now meditate on the fact that God has you here for a purpose. Ask him to give you assurance and to place genuine people around you who will encourage you to fulfill his plan.

Prayer Results:

_____

_____

_____

III. What if I had to pay for my salvation? Would I really be able to afford it, or would I have to be placed on a payment plan for life?

Meditate and focus on the word "free." Thank God for salvation and that you didn't have to pay for it in order to have it.

Prayer Results:

_____

_____

_____

IV. Faith is what you cannot see.

Now meditate on spiritual eyesight and not the physical eyesight. Then pray for God to help you become the faith walker he wants you to be.

Prayer Results:

_____

_____

_____

V. I cannot live without your new mercies you shower upon my life every morning.

Reflect on the brand-new mercies that God allows you to see every morning. Pray with lifted hands and thank him for many mercies.

Prayer Results:

_____

_____

_____

VI. *I need to be a blessing because, God, you have blessed me.*

Now meditate on ways that God has blessed you. Then pray and ask God to show you how and when to be a blessing to others.

Prayer Results:

_____

_____

_____

VII. *Your love is immeasurable toward me, God.*

Meditate on how you could never repay God for his unconditional love. Ask God to give you what it takes to love others like he loves you.

Prayer Results:

_____

_____

_____

VIII. *There is no one greater than you, my God. My worship and my praise belong to you.*

Now meditate on the greatness and awesomeness of God. Pray and tell him how grateful you really are.

Prayer Results:

_____

_____

_____

Help Me Make It Through Scriptures

LUCRETIA MASON-UNDERDUE

uote at least one of these scriptures before or after you pray. *(All scriptures are quoted from the New International Version of the Bible.)*

Isaiah 41:10 *"So do not fear, for I am with you; do not be dismayed, for I am your God. I will strengthen you and help you; I will uphold you with my righteous right hand."*

John 10: 14-15 *"I am the good Shepherd, I know my sheep and my sheep know me, just as the Father knows me and I know the Father; and I lay down my life for the sheep."*

Exodus 15:2 *"The LORD is my strength and my song; he has become my salvation. He is my God, and I will praise him, my father's God, and I will exalt him."*

John 15:13 *"Greater love hath no man than this: to lay down one's life for one's friends."*

Psalm 27:1 *"The LORD is my light and my salvation--whom shall, I fear? The LORD is the stronghold of my life--of whom shall I be afraid?"*

1 Chronicles 16:8 *"Give praise to the Lord, proclaim his name; make known among the nations what he has done."*

Psalm 118:24 *"The Lord has done it this very day; let us rejoice today and be glad."*

1 Chronicles 16:8 *"Oh give thanks to the LORD, call upon His name; Make known His deeds among the peoples."*

2 Corinthians 5:7 *"For we live by faith, and not by sight."*

Isaiah 41:13 *"For I am the Lord your God who takes hold of your right hand and says to you, Do not fear; I will help you."*

Matthew 5:16 *"In the same way, let your light shine before others, that they may see your good deeds and glorify your Father in heaven."*

Hebrews 11:6 *"And without faith it is impossible to please God, because anyone who comes to him must believe he exists and that he rewards those who earnestly seek him."*

Isaiah 6:8 *"Then I heard the voice of the Lord saying, "Whom shall I send? And who will go for us?" And I said, "Here am I. Send me!"*

Jeremiah 29:11 *"For I know the plans I have for you," declares the Lord, "plans to prosper you and not to harm you, plans to give you hope and a future."*

Psalm 30:5 *"For his anger lasts only a moment, but his favor lasts a lifetime; weeping may stay for the night but rejoicing comes in the morning."*

1 Corinthians 13:4-8 *"Love is patient, love is kind. It does not envy, it does not boast, it is not proud. It does not dishonor others, it is* not self-seeking, it is not easily angered, it keeps no record of wrongs. Love does not delight in evil but rejoices with the truth. It always protects, always trusts, always hopes, always perseveres. Love never fails. But where there are prophecies, they will cease; where there are tongues, they will be stilled; where there is knowledge, it will pass away."

Romans 8:28 *"And we know that in all things God works for the good of those who love him, who have been called according to his purpose."*

Psalm 27:14 *"Wait for the LORD; be strong and take heart and wait for the LORD."*

1 Chronicles 16:34 *"Give thanks to the LORD, for he is good; his love endures forever."*

Psalm 118:24 *"The Lord has done it this very day; let us rejoice today and be glad."*

Psalm 51:10 *"Create in me a pure heart, O God, and renew a steadfast spirit within me."*

John 8:36 *"So if the Son sets free, you will be free indeed."*

Proverbs 3:5 *"Trust in the LORD with all your heart and lean not on your own understanding; in all your ways submit to him, and he will make your paths straight."*

www.ingramcontent.com/pod-product-compliance
Lightning Source LLC
Chambersburg PA
CBHW071022080526
44587CB00015B/2464